CONTENTS

MILITARY 2·00

Pundits and Patriots

Lessons from the Gulf War

by
Philip Towle

Alliance Publishers Ltd., for the
INSTITUTE FOR EUROPEAN DEFENCE AND STRATEGIC STUDIES

First published 1991
© INSTITUTE FOR EUROPEAN DEFENCE AND STRATEGIC STUDIES

ISBN 0 907 967 24 8

Designed by Reginald Cline MCSD MSTD
Typeset by Typeright, Highbury, London
Printed by SR Press Ltd., Exeter

PREFACE

One of the most notable features of the Gulf War of 1990-1991 was the extent to which coverage of it was often dominated by instant comment from experts, whether politicians, retired military and diplomatic figures, academics or journalists. Although many commentators were responsible and moderate in thier statements, others predicted for example, that the conflict would develop into a third world war or result in either a nuclear exchange or the deployment of chemical weapons. A prolonged war, massive casualties and environmental disaster seemed imminent; a view which inevitably caused deep and unjustified anxiety to the families and friends of those serving in the allied forces.

Few commentators, by contrast, foresaw the speed with which Iraq would be routed, although there was ample evidence pointing to this as the most likely outcome.

In an uncertain situation, the pundits' views carried weight in much of Western Europe and the United States, and through their influence on public opinion might have had an effect on policy had events not so rapidly proved them wrong.

As Dr. Philip Towle, of Queens' College, Cambridge points out in this, the fiftieth occasional paper to be published by this Institute, the pundits' record in the war deserves scrutiny, not motivated by any wish to embarrass those whose judgements turned out to be wrong, but rather to explain why they thought as they did and why events did not unfold as they predicted.

All of the principal powers on the allied side in the Gulf had been defeated in a guerrilla war since 1945. Dr. Towle suggests that the difference between such insurgencies and the type of conventional war which was to be expected with Iraq, in which Western industrial and material superiority had a greater effect on the outcome, was frequently overlooked by the pessimists.

Too great significance was also placed on estimates of Iraqi strength from defence annuals and similar publications which, Dr Towle argues, encouraged the tendency to think only in terms of material and numbers, ignoring societal differences and the less easily definable characteristics of leadership, morale and training.

The likely effectiveness of what were expected to be Iraq's main responses to the allied assault, chemical warfare and random terrorism, was grossly overestimated by many experts. Iraq had gained little advantage from the use of chemical weapons on the ill-equipped Iranian forces. Such weapons might well have had the effect of hindering an allied advance because of the need for personnel to wear protective clothing, but they were never likely to inflict massive casualties on an invading force as they had on unprotected civilians.

Equally, terrorist attacks, on targets such as civil aircraft would, Dr. Towle asserts, have disrupted travel but would not have had any strategic significance or affected the resolve of allied governments to drive Iraq from Kuwait.

While exaggerating Iraqi capabilities, commentators were also prone to suggest that the very sophistication of much Western (and particularly American) equipment was a source of weakness. Some of it was untested in combat and would, it was alleged, be found wanting. In particular, the degree of precision with which air strikes can now be mounted, was not realised even by many respected observers, until the devastating effects of such attacks became apparent.

Dr. Towle puts forward a number of reasons why so many pundits were wrong either about the course or the outcome of the war. Anti-Western bias blinded the perception and judgement of some of them, especially Islamic fundamentalists. Others, such as Soviet military commentators, found it hard to accept that Iraq, whose forces had to a large extent been trained and equipped by the Soviet Union, could be so easily defeated. In the West, some of the most doom-laden predictions, Dr. Towle suggests, came from pacifists who continued to believe, in defiance of much of the evidence, that economic sanctions would eventually compel Saddam Hussein to give up Kuwait. The war also did much, he believes, to correct previous pessimistic assumptions, dating from the Vietnam War, about the capability and competence of the armed forces of the United States.

Above all perhaps, the lesson that Dr. Towle derives from the Gulf experience is that public opinion, in democratic states particularly, will respond to a strong and decisive lead from governments. To the extent that both government and public morale can be affected by the quality and accuracy of expert opinion, many commentators might profitably ponder on the hazards and pitfalls of military punditry as well as upon the strategic and political lessons of the actual conflict.

The Institute does not seek to express a corporate view, but we are grateful that in this fiftieth Occasional Paper, which represents a landmark in our own endeavours, Dr. Towle has provided a shrewd and incisive commentary on aspects of a conflict which may be seen in time as the foretaste of a new and unpredictable world order.

June 1991   AJM

1. INTRODUCTION

"Even the most optimistic military pundit has to accept that things are not going to plan...we will be lucky if the war is over in six months."
Dr Paul Rogers, Bradford University

The overwhelming victory of the anti-Iraq coalition in the Gulf War of January and February 1991 seems, in retrospect, to have been inevitable. By seizing the Emirate of Kuwait in August 1990, a Third World leader challenged the technological might of the United States and its allies. Iraq, a nation of perhaps 18 million, which had already suffered eight years of war against a more powerful neighbour and which had a gross domestic product of only 45 billion dollars, took on three major First World countries and a substantial group from the Third World. The outcome was a conflict in which the anti-Iraqi coalition devastated Baghdad's armed forces, inflicting tens of thousands of casualties, whilst suffering only a handful itself. In the immediate aftermath, the struggle had come to seem so unbalanced that anti-war spokesmen, such as Kalim Siddiqi, director of the Moslem Institute in London, took to ridiculing Western victory celebrations on the grounds that, "it was hardly a war - there was no contest in the air or on land".[1] The myth had already begun to gain ground in the Arab world that the US Administration had been certain of its vast superiority from the start and had consciously set out to destroy Iraq in order both to establish its own dominance over the international system and to help Israel.

But victory did not seem so inevitable or affordable beforehand, either to a section of the opinion-forming elite in the West or to large sections of the population in some

9

countries. All of the principal powers involved on the allied side had been defeated by Third World guerrilla movements: France in Algeria and Indo-China, Britain in Palestine and Aden, the Soviet Union in Afghanistan and, most spectacularly, the United States in Vietnam. Since guerrilla warfare is by far the most common form of conflict in the modern world, it was easy to forget that conventional wars are quite different from insurgencies and that the superiority of the Western industrial societies in this field is very firmly based.

Furthermore, Iraqi power rested not only on its conventional military forces but on its purported ability to unleash terrorist attacks on Western targets, to damage the environment, to encourage Arab peoples to overthrow governments hostile to Baghdad and to use weapons of mass destruction, such as chemical, biological and possibly even nuclear weapons. It was these alleged Iraqi strengths which encouraged some in the West to feel that the struggle would be far less ill-matched than it actually was.

Commentators from the elite also found it difficult to judge how the Western and Arab publics would weigh up the balance between Iraq and its enemies. The distinguished military historian, Sir Michael Howard of Yale University, argued in August 1990 that the United States should not force Iraq to leave Kuwait but wait for economic sanctions to persuade it to do so. The great danger was that "the Rambo elements in the United States and the "Gotcha" faction in (Britain would) provoke a military confrontation". The alternative to sanctions was a prolonged and disastrous war similar to the Korean conflict. By January 1991 Sir Michael had changed his mind because "the longer the western use of force is delayed, the less credible it becomes. Protest movements have begun to spread across America and are gathering strength. The American media, unable to distinguish between impartiality and irresponsibility, exploit every suggestion of poor morale among American forces in the Gulf..and make civilian flesh creep with tales of nerve gas and body bags".[2] The historian had thus moved in five months from fearing that the public would under-estimate Iraqi power to believing that it was over-estimating its power and the consequent dangers of war.

Given their victory over Argentina in 1982, the British people might have been expected to have been confident about the prospects of expelling the Iraqis from Kuwait. Certainly opinion polls showed very high levels of support for taking a strong line against Iraq, suggesting that the general public believed that Iraq could, if necessary, be defeated at acceptable cost. Yet Professor Paul Wilkinson of the University of St Andrews voiced the views of a section of the elite in January 1991, when he contrasted the Falklands War with the prospects of war with Iraq, and suggested that the second would be far more dangerous. He expected such a conflict to be "one of the most lethal wars since 1945...(with) a high possibility of weapons of mass destruction being used, with casualty estimates of one million civilians".[3] Wilkinson saw the war spreading across the Middle East and even strengthening conservative opposition to Mr Gorbachev in the Soviet Union.

The Falklands conflict was a far more difficult and dangerous military operation for Britain. It involved British forces fighting without allies at the end of supply lines which stretched back 8,000 miles across the Atlantic. In the air, British forces were vastly outnumbered and, if the Argentines had had bombs which could explode when released at low level, the losses suffered by British warships might have been decisive. Even on land the Argentines had superiority and weeks to prepare the ground. Nevertheless, the British armed forces achieved a decisive victory and did not suffer at all from the fact that Latin Americans were far more united in their opposition to Britain than the Arabs or Moslems were in support of Saddam Hussein nine years later.

11

II. A PAPER TIGER?

Assessing Iraqi Power

Why did some commentators - politicians, academics, journalists - regard Iraq as so much more formidable an enemy than Argentina had been in 1982? Firstly, Iraq was separated from Kuwait by only a few miles of sand rather than the hundreds of miles of stormy seas which divided Argentina and the Falklands. Once having absorbed their prey, both Argentina and Iraq had the three to one advantage which being on the defensive is usually said to provide against the attacker. But the Argentines had not fought a conventional war for decades, whilst, for the Iraqis, the eight years of war against Iran had produced what was expected to be a battle-hardened army of just under one million men. This compared with a United States Army of 760,000, a French Army of 288,000 and a British Army of 153,000. Iraq had fought much of the war against Iran behind fortifications and its army was considered to be expert in building up greats walls of mines, barbed wire and sand. It had also accumulated huge quantities of French and Soviet equipment. Without this it would have been unable to stem the attacks of the Iranians who had rebuffed the initial Iraqi attack in September 1980 and had then gone on the offensive for much of the war. Iran is a nation of 54 million people and its gross domestic product is seven times larger than Iraq's. Iran's forces also fought with the ferocity of revolutionaries and religious fanatics.

So the Iraqis relied on equipment to rebuff the Iranians and bought some 5,500 main battle tanks from the Soviet Union. Most of these were old T-55 and T-56s but they also had 1,500 more modern T-62 and T-72 tanks which equipped the crack "Republican Guard". To complement these, the Iraqi armed forces had bought thousands of field guns and 4,000 air defence guns. In the air they had over 500 combat aircraft including 70 MiG 23s, 25 MiG 25s and over 90 Mirage Fls.[4] They had also taken note of recent practice in Europe and elsewhere, building hardened aircraft shelters to protect their aircraft and constructing immense runways across the arid countryside. Most of this equipment was accurately listed in the International Institute for Strategic Studies' annual publication *The Military Balance* and by similar institutions elsewhere. The danger was that such publications inadvertently encouraged the tendency to think only in terms of material and numbers, ignoring the less definable characteristics of leadership, morale and training. Newspapers referred *en passant* to Iraq's lengthy battle experience against Iran and then dwelt on the fact that its armed forces were said to be the fourth largest in the world.

Secret Weapons

The belief that Iraq had "secret weapons", which it would spring on the allies to devastating effect, contributed to Western over-estimation of its capability. In December 1990 it was reported that Iraq was preparing trenches full of oil to be ignited if the allies attacked, and these were indeed discovered after its defeat. General Stanislav Petrov, Chief of the Soviet Chemical Troops, estimated that the Iraqis had between 2,000 and 4,000 tons of chemical weapons including mustard gas, prussic acid and the nerve agents, tabun and sarin. These exerted a fear out of all proportion to their military effectiveness. Professor Wilkinson suggested that they would be so effective that the allies might have to retaliate with nuclear weapons, whilst Dr Alastair Hay from Leeds University thought that allied protective equipment would be ineffective against a sustained attack.[5]

Yet chemical weapons had not been particularly destructive even against the ill-prepared Iranians and they would have been less so against allied forces. The main result of the threat of chemical warfare was to impose serious restraints on allied troops by compelling them to wear protective suits. Chemical weapons are an easy way of murdering unprotected civilians, as the Iraqis had proved against Kurdish villages. But for well-equipped soldiers it is far better to have a chemical, rather than an ordinary high explosive, shell land close at hand.

There were also suggestions that the Iraqis might have nuclear weapons. Iraq was certainly trying to develop a nuclear force but it was years from achieving one. Its main nuclear reactor, bought from France, had been destroyed by Israeli aircraft on 7 June 1981. It had a number of small research reactors but there was no hard evidence that it had constructed a reprocessing plant. Since American public opinion was particularly anxious that the Iraqi nuclear capability should be destroyed, it seems likely that US officials allowed stories of Iraq's nuclear capability to circulate in order to harden public resolve.

The alternative Jeremiad spread by the former British Prime Minister, Edward Heath and by Paul Wilkinson, was that the allies would suffer so decisive a defeat at the hands of the Iraqis that they would have to use nuclear weapons. Fears were also stoked by newspaper headlines warning that, "the scale of nuclear firepower (in the Gulf) threatens holocaust". Such reports suggested that each US aircraft carrier in the region might be carrying 120 nuclear weapons, though the probability was that these had been unloaded to make room for conventional weapons. They were irrelevant to the conflict in hand and would have caused serious difficulties if the ships had been sunk. The British and Americans had told the UN formally in 1978 that they would never use nuclear weapons against a state which did not have such weapons, unless the latter were attacking them in concert with a nuclear armed state. Heath's vision vastly exaggerated both Iraqi power and the likely allied response to it.[6]

Fears were increased by the fact that Iraq possessed a number of ballistic missiles. Communist countries had been selling old surface to surface missiles to Middle Eastern countries for some time and these had been widely used in the Iran-Iraq War. The Scud B missiles, which both Iran and Iraq had in their arsenals, dated from the mid 1960s and were too inaccurate to hit anything but large cities. Even then they could only be really effective if they were armed with chemical warheads. It was unclear, however, whether Iraq had succeeded in arming them in this way and whether Western anti-ballistic missiles would be capable of intercepting them. In the event, Iraq did not use chemical warheads against Israel or Saudi Arabia, although it did launch a number of missiles. The US Patriot missile proved capable of intercepting a substantial proportion of the Scuds launched, though it did not give total protection. The real political importance of the Scud offensive was that it might have encouraged Israel to attack Iraq and thus made it even more difficult for such Arab states as Syria and Egypt to remain within the anti-Iraqi coalition. Under allied pressure, the Israelis decided to remain neutral, despite the attacks upon them.

Iraq's "secret weapons" were confined to ecocide, terrorism and the manipulation of hostages. Saddam Hussein's decision in August 1990 to intern Western citizens living in Kuwait and to spread some of them around his military installations, was a very serious breach of international law. It was also the first time in Twentieth Century history that such a ploy had been openly tried on any scale. But Hussein lacked the will to maintain it. By first taking and then releasing the hostages, he succeeded in outraging the West without giving Iraq any extra protection. Professor Raju Thomas of Marquette University, Wisconsin wrote afterwards in the Singapore *Straits Times*, "Those hostages ensured more effectively that the lives of thousands of innocent Iraqi men, women and children would be protected from American strategic bombing.

Their release has produced war and not prevented it".[7] It is certainly true that, if the Iraqis had kept Western hostages, the bombing campaign in January and February 1991, which prepared the way for the allied ground offensive, would have been more complicated. The allies would have tried to find where they were being held and to avoid those particular targets. It is most unlikely, however, that they would have avoided war altogether, as Professor Thomas suggested. Indeed the allies would probably have been even more determined to defeat Iraq. Public opinion has learnt from previous hostage crises and backed governments' refusal to negotiate with captors.

The Threat of Terror

During the long crisis, the terrorist threat by Iraq proved damaging economically but ineffective politically. In September 1990 the terrorist leader, Abul Abbas warned in Baghdad that "we will use any method to defend ourselves....if the United States sends aircraft to bomb Baghdad then that is terror". In the same month, George Habash, the leader of the Popular Front for the Liberation of Palestine, declared that "at this moment our fingers are touching the trigger. We will start the moment Iraq suffers aggression".[8] In January, Iraqi diplomats sent home from Britain warned that Moslems living there would take their revenge. One unfortunate result was that any who seemed suspicious were rounded up and either detained or deported. The number of people using British airports fell by 20 per cent, holiday bookings declined by as much as 80 per cent and great numbers of flights, particularly across the Atlantic, were cancelled.[9] Travellers evidently had little faith in the ability of airlines to give adequate protection. The destruction of a Pan American aircraft over Lockerbie in December 1988 has had a particularly strong impact on the public imagination and vastly more money will have to be spent over the next decade installing more effective equipment for searching baggage before the public will be reassured.

16

Many were surprised that the Iraqis and the terrorist groups which supported them did not stage a major terrorist coup during the war itself. There are a number of possible explanations for their failure to do so. One is that such coups take months of preparation and none may have been complete by the end of the war. Another is that great efforts were being made by Western Intelligence services to forestall terrorist incidents. In particular Iraqi diplomats who might otherwise have transported bombs and other weapons were placed under close surveillance. Finally there were reports afterwards that the Syrians, as partners in the anti-Iraqi coalition, had helped to prevent Iraqi terrorism.[10] Given the way that groups backed by Libya, Syria and Iraq have co-operated together in the past, the Syrians may well have been sufficiently informed about potential terrorists to reduce the threat they presented. The public suspected that terrorists would attack airliners, but this did not change their mind about government policy. A successful attack of this kind would have had a traumatic effect on public opinion without, however, affecting the course of the war.

Iraqi efforts to destroy the environment were more innovative and far more dangerous. Before the war began, environmentalist groups in Britain correctly predicted that, if they were attacked, the Iraqis would blow up the Kuwaiti oilfield. John Cox, an independent consultant to the oil industry, suggested at the beginning of January 1991 that the resulting fires would affect the climate and particularly the Asian monsoon. Similarly Edward Heath said that the oil fires would push the temperature in Kuwait up to 60 degrees Centigrade and make it impossible for the Saudis to work their wells. Experts disagreed about these predictions and whether the invaders would take this course.[11] In the event, the Iraqis did blow up the oilfields but the effects were not exactly those predicted. The temperature in the area did not rise dramatically and Indian experts felt that the monsoon would not be affected. However the Kuwaiti Oil Company estimated that the fires consumed even more oil than anticipated and the fumes given off were a serious threat to the health of people living in the Gulf. Moreover, the Iraqis had further damaged the environment by releasing massive oil slicks into the sea and the military vehicles concentrated in the area broke up the topsoil and increased the number of sandstorms.[12]

Environmental warnings were thus the only ones given by the anti-war group of British Members of Parliament, led by Edward Heath, Denis Healey and Tam Dalyell, or the anti-war movement in the USA led by Zbigniew Brzezinski, which proved to be justified. Yet, even if the allies had known the worst beforehand, it is difficult to see how this would have altered their plans. If ecocide were shown to be an effective strategy, then every future invader would threaten to carry it out in order to deter a counter-attack. The environmentalists are in the difficult position that the more they stress the dangers, the more those dangers are likely to become real.

III. THE PERILS OF PREDICTION

Excessive Pessimism

It was difficult for political and military leaders to give accurate guidance to the public about what the war might bring. They did not want to be accused during or after the war of "selling" it to the people by minimising the dangers. Right up to the end, therefore, they cautioned against excessive optimism and thousands of hospital beds were prepared, both in the battle zone and in Britain. The US Defense Secretary, Richard Cheney dismissed the precise casualty estimates which some had put forward: "We've tried to be honest and say what we know. And if we don't know we have stated that very precisely".[13] There is no evidence to suggest that allied leaders were certain of the "casualty-free" victory for their forces which eventually took place and the media quoted estimates of casualties ranging into the tens of thousands.

The general line taken by military officers serving in the Gulf, when briefing the press, was that the struggle would be fierce but that allied victory was certain. Captain Brent Beecham of the US Air Force, who had studied the Iraqi regime and armed forces for some years, argued that the allies would succeed in the air because of the inferiority of Iraqi aircraft and the inflexibility of their tactics.[14] In August, British Intelligence sources correctly pointed out that many of the Iraqi troops along the Saudi frontier were ill-trained teenagers.[15] In November, British commanders said that they were confident of breaching the defences which the Iraqis had built along their frontiers.[16] Just before the ground war began, the commander of the 7th British Armoured Brigade in Saudi Arabia forecast that it was "going to be noisy, its going to be frightening and....chaotic". But he also thought the war would be short and that the allies would be victorious.[17]

Newspaper reports suggested that Intelligence analysts in the USA were more pessimistic. Excerpts from a US Army War College study concluded that "the (Iraqi) Army has high institutional self-esteem, morale is good after the victory over Iran....Officers are well trained and confident".[18] It is difficult to tell whether the selections published fully reflected the report but the suggestion that Iraq had been victorious against Iran was certainly surprising. The US Deputy Chief of Staff for Intelligence also prepared a handbook for the US forces in the Gulf which was partly leaked to the press. It seemed to suggest that the Iraqi Army was "one of the best-equipped and most combat experienced in the world...distinguished by its flexibility, unity of command and high level of mobility". The report apparently praised Iraqi logistics and maintenance, though suggesting that curbs on commanders' initiative reduced the efficiency of the army.[19]

The size of the Iraqi forces stationed on the Saudi frontier also seems to have been exaggerated by allied Intelligence. The Iraqi government in Baghdad was constantly boasting about the size of its army and this may have influenced calculations. The allies allegedly added up the number of divisions in the area without taking account of the possibility that they could be seriously under strength. Thus the coalition expected to meet 540,000 Iraqi troops, although there may only have been 350,000 in the battle zone.[20]

A Baroque Arsenal?

The over-estimation of the size and capability of Iraqi forces in these reports was compounded amongst outside experts by under-estimation of US strength. Not only were the US armed forces associated with defeats in Vietnam, Iran and Lebanon but a number of academics had been arguing for some time that the US armed forces relied too heavily on expensive and sophisticated equipment that would not work in battle. The distinguished American strategist, Edward Luttwak warned President Bush against using force because "the resulting casualties could easily destroy the Bush presidency". Luttwak believed that the Iraqis were "too combat-experienced to run under fire". Furthermore their weapons were simple and effective while the US was concentrating on "fanciful tactics, flashy weapons and promising gadgets that seem fine in peace-time exercises but fail in combat". In February 1991 Luttwak argued that fighting could be avoided altogether on the ground if allied aircraft concentrated on cutting the supply routes to the Iraqi Army. In his view the allies suffered because the campaign was commanded by an Army officer, General Schwarzkopf, and the Chairman of the US Chiefs of Staff, Colin Powell, was also an Army officer. They did not understand, Luttwak asserted, that bombing the Iraqi Army itself, rather than its supply lines, was an inefficient use of air power.[21]

During the war, Luttwak's articles were given prominence in the London press. The debate on US technology had long since spread to Europe. It had been the subject of the conference held by the International Institute for Strategic Studies in 1984 when Dr Stephen Canby led the attack on Western over-reliance on complex, long-range weaponry. However, the most provocative and widely read critique of modern conventional technology to appear in Britain was *The Baroque Arsenal* by Mary Kaldor of Sussex University which was published in 1982. This diverged from the Luttwak line in being relatively sympathetic to precision-guided missiles, which Ms Kaldor argued had made tanks and aircraft obsolete. On the whole, however, she believed that many modern weapons are "incapable of achieving limited military objectives... sophisticated weapons are difficult to handle; they go wrong; they need thousands of spare parts". This became, in fact, the refrain of those advocating an "alternative" defence strategy in the 1980s. NATO should abandon its nuclear weapons, tanks and aircraft, and arm itself with

21

defensive weapons, such as anti-tank and anti-aircraft missiles. It is difficult to see how this could have solved the coalition's problems when dealing with Iraq in 1991. What were needed to expel the invaders from Kuwait were long-range aircraft and powerful tanks, equipped with precision-guided munitions. Certainly many of the coalition's weapons did go wrong, as Luttwak, Kaldor, Canby and others predicted, but the allies had plenty of time to prepare for the conflict and, after these careful preparations, the weapons proved sufficiently "unbaroque" to achieve the limited objectives set.[22]

The Cost of War

Many others, including some of the British politicians who participated in the debate, stressed the great price which would have to be paid for a coalition victory, rather than the dangers of defeat. In particular they argued that thousands of Kuwaitis would be killed in any battle. According to Denis Healey, the former British Minister of Defence, "it is very doubtful if one building would be left standing in Kuwait. The war that the United States is planning to fight would probably mean the death by bombing of almost every man, woman and child living in Kuwait city at least".[23] Similarly, the analyst Elizabeth Young, wrote to *The Independent*, "although some strategists believe in the possibility of a 'surgical strike' against highly specific Iraqi targets, experience in Grenada, Libya and Panama, where targets were virtually undefended, suggests otherwise. Such a campaign would most likely trigger a wider war". The Medical Campaign Against Nuclear Weapons warned at the beginning of 1991 that the National Health Service in Britain would be flooded with 300,000 casualties including 60,000 which would be fatal. It predicted that there would be a million civilian casualties in the Gulf including 100,000 deaths.[24]

Naturally, journalists working in Saudi Arabia made differing predictions about how a war might turn out. Many simply reported and reflected military views. Some were optimistic and some pessimistic. Robert Fisk of *The Independent* was one of the most experienced Middle East correspondents but, in the event, his reports gave his readers much too pessimistic a view of the ensuing battle. It was Fisk who published the US Intelligence report on the efficiency of the Iraqi Army, though on a later occasion he criticised the allies' Intelligence organisations for being too optimistic. In December 1990, he stressed the difficulties that the allied armies would encounter in co-ordinating any offensive, concluding that, "as so often before, General Disorder could turn out to be the overall commander". In January 1991 he wrote, "anyone who believes in the myth of the short, sharp victory should drive up the road to the Kuwaiti frontier", where the allies were preparing thousands of hospital beds for the expected casualties.[25]

Soviet Views

In estimating Iraqi power it was not unreasonable for the Western elites to take account of the views of those Egyptians and Soviets who had been training the Iraqi armed forces and who might be expected to have formed an accurate impression of their capability. Unfortunately, Soviet views were also misleading because they were over-confident about Iraqi military effectiveness. The Chief of the Operations Research Centre of the Soviet General Staff, Sergei Bogdanov, simply said that "Baghdad has a substantial enough military arsenal to inflict tangible losses on the enemy". Major General Kostin, a professor at the General Staff Academy, was more forthcoming. Before the land war began, he argued:

"the allied forces are opposed on land by a million strong Iraqi army, well-equipped and toughened in the war against Iran. Iraqi units are patently superior to their enemy in combat skills in desert conditions. They have some well-organised defence positions which it won't be easy to seize even in the event of air supremacy. Soviet-made T62 and T72 tanks are more adapted to operation in a desert than the US M-1 Abrams. Moreover, the tanks are well dug in and it won't be easy to get at them, even with high precision weapons".[26]

Kostin predicted a long war of positions, similar to the Iran-Iraq War. Many Soviet generals were still more optimistic about Iraq's chances. Major General Victor Filatov, Editor in Chief of the Soviet *Journal of Military History*, was amongst the most outspoken of these. At the beginning of February 1991 he dismissed Western success in the air as little more than propaganda directed by Western officials.

"The United States is steadily driving its nation towards a second Vietnam, which will be much worse than the first one. The Vietnamese were not living throughout the world, while Arabs and Moslems are. As soon as the land war starts, governments in Syria and Egypt may begin swaying....Even if Iraq is defeated, which I doubt, other Arab nations will join the war against the so-called coalition forces".[27]

This was a point made by General Mikhail Moiseyev, the chief Soviet military commander in September 1990 when he warned that Iran might join Iraq and that their combined efforts would be powerful enough to lead to a third world war.[28]

In retrospect it is easy to see that the "wish was father to the thought". Soviet officers had a vested interest in their equipment and believed that it could match its Western equivalent successfully. Afterwards, with some justification, many blamed Iraqi incompetence for their defeat. Others thought that a combination of factors was responsible. Colonel Alexander Tsalk, who headed a Soviet Air Force training centre before he was elected to the assembly, argued that the war showed the uselessness of deploying vast numbers of tanks which could be destroyed from the air. On the other hand, Colonel Nikolai Petrushenko, who led the pro-Iraq group in the assembly, argued that allied success had been deliberately exaggerated by Western propagandists. In his view, "only a very naive person" could believe that the allies merely lost 70 people during the month long war.[29]

In the same debate the Defence Minister, Marshal Dimitri Yazov, admitted that the war demonstrated the need for a review of the Soviet army's defence systems, though he claimed that they had destroyed 93 allied fighters. On another occasion, Yazov argued that the Iraqi aircraft were so outnumbered that they had had no chance to prove themselves. At the same time, he pointed out, Soviet-made T-62 tanks in the Syrian army had fought alongside the coalition forces. These had proved more reliable than the American Abrams tanks which had trouble with their sand filters.[30] However Yazov was fighting a complicated political battle and his comments evidently reflected that. He wanted to avoid demoralising the Soviet armed forces whilst putting pressure on his colleagues in the Soviet government to keep up defence expenditure, particularly in the sphere of research and development. His true feelings may thus have been masked.[31]

Many officers disliked the West and hoped to see it humiliated. Filatov, in particular, appeared to relish the prospect of the West encountering "another Vietnam". The Soviet armed forces reflected the views of a considerable number of Soviet citizens, a number of whom wrote in the Soviet journal *New Times* offering to fight for Iraq. Some were Moslems who said they wanted to drive the "impudent Kaffirs" from the Holy Land but many were ordinary citizens who hated the West. Naturally the Iraqi government also tried to impress Soviet delegations throughout the crisis with their country's power. Five representatives of Soviet organisations who went to Baghdad in October 1990 were shown "a rehearsal of a million-strong parade of the people's army. The parade opened with a march of a womens' battalion followed by units of volunteers from Arab countries and detachments of *Kamikaze* fighters in black clothes". The delegates duly relayed their impressions to the Russian people.[32]

The Egyptians had also trained the Iraqi Army but, unlike the Soviets, they sent troops to join the anti-Iraqi coalition. They were not, however, responsible for Iraqi armaments and they took a much more pessimistic view of Iraqi prospects. Field Marshal Ghazala, the former Defence Minister, forecast in December 1990 that allied air forces would quickly gain control of the skies and that the Iraqi Army would then be easily defeated. He thought that the troops were poorly trained and that Saddam Hussein had killed the most enterprising senior officers because they presented a threat to his position. In January 1991, a senior Egyptian officer was quoted as saying, "there will be an air attack, then a ground attack and sweeping up". He forecast that the whole campaign would take about three weeks.[33] The Egyptians had far more to lose than the Soviets, if their forecasts were inaccurate, so their estimates should have merited the closest attention.

Iraq's leaders, and particularly Saddam Hussein himself, naturally set out to give the impression that the Iraqi armed forces would win because of their courage and self sacrifice. Before the war began, he told April Glaspie, the US Ambassador to Iraq; "I do not belittle you. But I hold this view by looking at the geography and nature of American society....Yours is a society which cannot accept 10,000 dead in battle".[34] No doubt he was influenced by the lessons of the Vietnam War, in which the loss of some 50,000 men and the savagery of the fighting had eventually led many Americans to demand the end of the war. Subsequent military disasters, such as the abortive attempt to rescue US hostages in Iran and the killing of US Marines by a terrorist car bomb in Beirut, had created a general climate of scepticism in the United States about the capacity of the armed forces. Thus, until fighting actually began, there was doubt about whether a majority of the American people would give it their support. The Iraqis were only too well aware of this uncertainty and may have relied upon it to prevent a US-led attack on their forces.

In the Gulf War US commanders knew that they were fighting to restore the reputation of their respective services. They were very sensitive about losing men and they waged war in a way designed to minimise their own casualties, noting that it was losses in limited wars, such as Vietnam and the Gulf, which most influenced the public mood. President Bush had to prove that the United States could fight without massive casualties and still win the war. As he put it afterwards, "By God, we have kicked the Vietnam syndrome once and for all".[35]

It was not unreasonable for Saddam Hussein to doubt that the American public would support a long and bloody war and this may have been the decisive factor in his defiance of the coalition. Some of the same views about the United States had been current in Japan in the 1930s and had led to the attack on Pearl Harbor in December 1941. It was to encourage their own people and frighten the Americans that the Iraqi Revolutionary Command Council expressed "its deep faith and determination to achieve victory. Let everyone understand that this battle is going to become the mother and father of all battles". Just before the allied ground offensive in February 1991, the Iraqi army newspaper claimed that "the people of Iraq and the army are waiting and preparing for the great offensive and confident that they will emerge victorious".[36]

In the event of war, Saddam Hussein and his government may have hoped that their forces would hold out for months or years against the allies, as they had against the Iranians. He was reported as saying in September 1990, "we have fought for eight years (against Iran) and can fight for three, four, for six years more if we have to". A long war would certainly have placed great strains on the coalition, dividing Western public opinion and probably increasing opposition to pro-allied rulers in the Moslem world. The Voice of Baghdad radio constantly encouraged Egyptians and others to rise against their governments, "to vindicate the Arabs and Muslims". [37]

Many Moslem experts in Britain believed that the Arab peoples would listen to Baghdad radio. They constantly warned that so great was the hatred of Israel and the West, that governments which joined the coalition would be overthrown by their own peoples. This in turn worried Western commentators, such as Zbigniew Brzezinski, Paul Wilkinson and Denis Healey. According to Healey, "it could lead to a Jihad through the whole of the Muslim world from Morocco to Indonesia, which would sweep away the Arab regimes that are friendly to the West". This took no account of the views of Egypt's President Mubarak and others, who had far more to lose and totally disagreed with the pessimists' forecasts. The wishes of the Moslem experts were once again father to the thought. Though there were disturbances in Cairo and elsewhere, no pro-allied government was overthrown or seriously threatened by popular disturbances during the conflict.[38]

In the event, Iraqi propaganda convinced those Arabs who wanted to believe it. The Palestinians in particular hoped to see the United States humbled and Saddam Hussein leading a crusade to destroy Israel. Some Palestinians living in Kuwait co-operated with the Iraqi invaders on the assumption that Kuwait had become a permanent province of Iraq. After the end of hostilities, the whole Palestinian community in the Emirate paid a terrible price for their error. The Palestinians were misled by some of their own leaders who allowed emotion to cloud their judgement believing that the Iraqis would win the war. King Hussein of Jordan bowed to the wishes of his people and permitted his government to appear pro-Iraqi. He and his people thereby alienated the Saudis and others who had been Jordan's principal economic backers in the past.[39]

IV. WAYS AND MEANS

The Sanctions Argument

Those in the West who opposed the use of military force against Iraq, often argued that they were not indifferent to the plight of the Kuwaitis who were being raped, tortured and murdered by the invading troops. Instead they maintained that the Iraqis could (eventually) be forced to leave by other means. Iraq, it was said, was a "date and oil" republic whose military strength was disproportionate to its narrow economic base. It was on this economic weakness that the allies were recommended to focus their attention. Thus, according to Mary Kaldor, "we had a chance to liberate Kuwait through the pressure of sanctions and international public opinion". Similarly, according to Denis Healey, the allies should have given sanctions at least a year to work.[40] Ever since the First World War pacifists have hoped that sanctions would replace war as a means of bringing pressure to bear upon aggressors. The historical record hardly supports the contention that sanctions are effective, as they have never forced a dictator to back down when he was fully and publicly committed to a policy. In 1941 they simply pushed the Japanese towards war and more recently sanctions proved totally ineffective as a form of protest against such events as the Soviet invasion of Afghanistan in 1979.

Not only are sanctions rarely effective, they can also be far more destructive than their advocates usually admit. Those who supported sanctions as a way of bringing pressure to bear upon Iraq were rarely clear about whether they were prepared to starve it into surrender. Some suggested that food shortages would compel the civilian population to rise up against Saddam Hussein, without explaining how half-starved people were supposed to do this. When sanctions were imposed in August 1990, *The*

Times reported that, "a shortage of consumer goods could be felt first within a few weeks. The effect on food supplies will be slower, but possibly more damaging. Baghdad is estimated to have stores of grain for about six months". A week later, the same newspaper suggested that, as the Iraqi food supply had previously been one of the highest in the Middle East, considerable cuts in consumption were possible. The Iraqis introduced rationing in September and imposed the death penalty for hoarders two months later. They temporarily increased meat consumption by encouraging farmers to slaughter their animals.[41]

The Independent's correspondent in Baghdad also produced a series of reports on the effect of sanctions. By November he reported, "while it is easy to demonstrate that Iraqi society and the economy are being seriously affected by sanctions, there is no sign that they will crack in 1990 and very little that they will do so in 1991. As the months pass without a war, Iraqis who thought the invasion of Kuwait a dangerous gamble are beginning to wonder if President Saddam Hussein will not get away with it". After the fighting was over, the UN sent a mission under the Finnish diplomat Martti Ahtisaari to assess conditions in Iraq and see whether sanctions should be ended. The members of the mission argued that the combination of sanctions and war had indeed brought the country to the brink of starvation.[42] But such a report still leaves unclear whether economic measures on their own would have caused starvation. Even if they had done so, it is almost inconceivable that Saddam Hussein's government would have responded by changing its policy before television photographs of the starving had undermined the resolve of the coalition.

The problems with sanctions were compounded by the fact that the Iraqis could have starved the Kuwaitis, Kurds and foreigners living in their country before they allowed their own people to suffer. As it was, the US Defense Secretary, Richard Cheney, told the House Armed Services Committee on 14 December that he doubted whether sanctions would work and that force would have to be used.[43] It is still unclear whether any members of the Bush administration ever imagined that sanctions on their own would be effective. They may simply have been a way of sending signals to Baghdad about the gravity with which the seizure of Kuwait was viewed, and convincing public opinion in the allied countries that something was being done while the military build-up took place.

Superior Intelligence

Why then were the allies militarily successful when it became clear that sanctions would not succeed? They had one major advantage which became more apparent as the conflict progressed - a massive superiority in the collection of Intelligence. The West had been thwarted by terrorist movements for so long that America's strength in technological Intelligence was often forgotten. US reconnaissance satellites provided a very clear picture of Iraqi military dispositions and their efforts to fortify their frontiers and American radio monitoring services were also able to add to this picture. During the Gulf War itself, and possibly beforehand, allied special forces operated deep inside Iraqi territory, providing the allies with further information about Iraqi strength. To set against this, the Iraqis could only monitor the world press and make use of information from sympathetic outsiders. Whether this included information from some elements in the Soviet Union was uncertain but, in any case, it did little to balance the overwhelming US advantage.

Air Power Comes of Age

The second major reason for allied success was that air power had finally come of age. From when it was first used in combat before the Great War until the development of precision guided munitions, it had normally been a blunt instrument, having rightly developed a reputation for killing and terrorising civilians. The Germans had tried to use it in this way against British cities in the First

31

World War and the theorists of air power, Douhet, Trenchard and others, openly argued in the inter-war period that it should be used in attacks on civilians. The inability of bombers to hit precise targets meant that they were used primarily to try to break the will of civilians living in major cities, even though demoralised ordinary citizens could do nothing to force their governments to make peace.[44] The butchery had some economic effects and it diverted military efforts to home defence but until the development of nuclear weapons it was politically irrelevant.

The US experience of bombing North Vietnam was different in two important ways. First, no other single factor disillusioned so many with the war and so lowered America's reputation world-wide.[45] Second, towards the end of the war, the US introduced precision-guided munitions which, for the first time, made it possible to use aircraft as rapiers rather than bludgeons. The full effect of this development was hidden from the public. Nor were they enlightened by the US attack on Tripoli in 1986. On that occasion, the F lll bombers were ordered to attack at too low a level for the Pave Tac guided bombs to work effectively, with the result that the bombs fell off target and caused civilian casualties. [46]

During the war with Iraq, the US was able to use aircraft and guided missiles from warships to destroy key parts of Iraq's infrastructure. Coalition leaders may have hoped to force Saddam Hussein to come to terms even without using their ground forces. Alternatively, they may have hoped that the Iraqi armed forces would turn on their master when they saw what disaster he had brought upon them. Power stations, bridges, oil refineries, government ministries and communications facilities, all fell before the allied strikes. The coalition believed that the destruction of Iraqi communications would prepare the way for the ground attack, if the Iraqis proved unbending. And this was the case, as Hussein showed that he preferred to see his country's economy destroyed piecemeal, rather than give up Kuwait.

The bombing offensive was still by no means as accurate and "casualty-free" as the allies would have preferred. Only 6,250 tons out of the total of 88,500 dropped were precision-guided. There were also failures both of technology and intelligence. Early in the campaign the allies bombed a factory making powder for babies' milk under the mistaken impression that it was also producing chemical or biological weapons. Richard Beeston of *The Independent* reported on 9 February 1991 that he had seen a military convoy which had been bombed near the city of Nasiriya, "most of the casualties appear to have been civilians caught among military vehicles. Elsewhere houses, pedestrians, and civilian motorists had been hit by air strikes intended to knock out bridges and other strategic sites". Refugees from Kuwait and elsewhere reported that their houses had been destroyed by allied bombs. Bombs from an RAF Tornado also hit civilians in the town of Fallujah in Iraq because they fell outside the laser beams which were supposed to guide them towards a bridge.[47] On other occasions, Iraqi anti-aircraft fire hit Tomahawk missiles fired from US warships and deflected them on to civilians.

Civilian Targets

Worst of all, on 13 February 1991, US bombs hit a bunker full of civilians.[48] The published evidence suggests that the bunker may have been used both as an air raid shelter and as a communications centre. Western Intelligence was aware of the second use but not of the first, and some hundreds of civilians were killed. The full total of civilian deaths in the campaign may never be known, because the Iraqis' own figures cannot be relied upon and it is quite possible that no accurate count was kept. All one can say is that the allies made great efforts to keep the total to a minimum and that without modern weapons such a campaign would have been impossible.

The allies' ability to mount precision attacks made it possible to contemplate attacking Saddam Hussein and his government directly. This notion was broached in public by the head of the US Air Force, General Duggan, early in the war. At the time it was too controversial and Duggan was sacked, but the possibility was regularly aired in the press. The allies had no mandate from the UN to overrun Iraq, but they wanted to be rid of the Iraqi leader and his death in an air attack would have been highly convenient. Critics suggested that such an attack was tantamount to assassination. However there is a distinction between murdering statesmen in peacetime and trying to destroy them in war. Battles in the past, such as those of Hastings and Bosworth, ended precisely when the enemy leader was killed or captured. It was only the tendency of leaders to avoid the battlefield in later centuries which protected them from attack. Ethically, there seems to be no reason to avoid attacking national leaders, who are directly responsible for the conflict, whilst killing civilians, or even soldiers, whose personal responsibility is negligible.

If modern weapons give air power the ability to be precise, they also enable it to be highly destructive. This was demonstrated during the other part of the air campaign which was waged against the Iraqi army and particularly its tanks. Many allied aircraft, such as the A 10, had been specifically designed to destroy tanks and 3,700 out of the 4,280 tanks in the Kuwait area were allegedly destroyed. The allies also made use of strategic bombers, such as the B52, which could "carpet bomb" a whole area and demolish everything in it. The Iraqis could reply with their anti-aircraft guns and a number of low flying aircraft were destroyed, but the allies had total air superiority. After the first weeks of the air campaign, what was left of the Iraqi Air Force fled to Iran. Edward Luttwak was simply wrong in his claim that the pounding of the Iraqi Army was an inefficient way to use air power. On the contrary, it proved enormously effective. His alternative suggestion that aircraft should have attacked food convoys would undoubtedly have led to more controversy, more civilian dead and more suffering amongst Kuwaiti civilians.

The allies were unsure about the effect of weeks of air attacks on Iraqi material and morale. Some drew parallels with the First World War and pointed out that massive artillery bombardments had never managed to destroy enough entrenched infantry to allow attacks to proceed very far. There were accounts from deserters stressing the efficacy of air attacks but at the time it was uncertain how typical they were of the army as a whole.[49] The bombing killed tens of thousands of Iraqi troops and left most of the others in no condition to fight. The allies were then criticised for being too destructive, contradicting earlier views about Iraqi strength and scepticism about the likely effectiveness of bombing.

The "Air-Land" Concept

Over the previous decade the United States had developed a new concept of highly mobile "air-land" warfare. Ground forces were given greater flexibility to use their initiative and strike deep into enemy territory. The aim was "securing or retaining the initiative and exercising it aggressively to defeat the enemy. Destruction of the opposing forces is achieved by throwing the enemy off balance with powerful initial blows from unexpected directions and then following up rapidly to prevent his recovery. Deep battle prevents the enemy from massing and creates windows of opportunity for offensive actions that allow us to defeat him in detail".[50] Luttwak dismissed such concepts as "fancy" and they certainly did rely on excellent communications which were particularly difficult to organise in the heterogeneous allied army. The six months before the crisis erupted into war were therefore immensely beneficial because they allowed some of these difficulties to be minimised. Thus, in addition to superior Intelligence and airpower, the new allied tactics and weapons were the crucial factor which threw the Iraqi armies into confusion and enabled the allies to win the war quickly and (from their own point of view) relatively bloodlessly.

IV. A GAME OF CARDS

Reasons to Differ

A "post mortem" on the predictions which were made about the outcome of the Gulf War is not an occasion for ridiculing those whose forecasts proved inaccurate. Many pessimists were motivated by the laudable humanitarian concern to avoid a disaster on the scale of the Korean and Vietnam Wars. In any case, there were many reasons for "experts" to differ. War is never an exact science. Carl von Clausewitz, the author of the most significant book ever written about warfare, concluded after a lifetime spent observing war or meditating on it,

"No other human activity is so continuously or universally bound up with chance. And through the element of chance, guesswork and luck come to play a great part in war....In short, absolute, so-called mathematical factors never find a firm basis in military calculations. From the very start there is an interplay of possibilities, probabilities, good luck and bad that weaves its way throughout the length and breadth of the tapestry. In the whole range of human activities, war most closely resembles a game of cards".[51]

Basic Miscalculations

Before the outbreak of fighting, the most common failings of commentators were to exaggerate:.

- Iraqi conventional military power (this was particularly common amongst Soviet commentators but was also widespread in the West).

36

- The weakness of US military technology (suggested by some Western commentators and journalists).
- The weakness of conservative Arab states and the hatred of Moslem peoples for the West (claimed by Moslem commentators in the West and elsewhere).
- The inefficiency and inaccuracy of air power (asserted by Western academic commentators).
- The power of terrorist movements to influence a conventional campaign (claimed by the terrorists themselves and some Western academics).
- The importance of chemical and biological warfare (stressed by Western academic writers and politicians, influencing the general public).
- The volatility of the oil market and the threat of price increases posed by a temporary loss of capacity (predicted by Western journalists and politicians).
- The state of Iraq's nuclear capability (speculated on by Western academic writers, probably encouraged by Western and Israeli officials).
- The efficacy and moral attractiveness of economic sanctions (propagated by Western academics and politicians).

A Fateful Gamble

Commentators may have had nothing to lose except their reputation for prescience but many of those actually involved were playing for very high stakes indeed. If some of the analyses of the Moslem world had proved correct, then most of the conservative leaders in the Middle East would have paid for their miscalculations with their positions and possibly their lives. In the West, Presidents Bush and Mitterand and Prime Ministers Thatcher and Major also gambled their futures on the outcome of the conflict.[52] Had the coalition been defeated, President Bush's

37

term of office might well have ended in an ignominy similar to that which marked the conclusion of the Johnson presidency.

The fate of whole peoples was at stake, and if the more pessimistic environmental calculations had proved correct, then the lives of vast numbers of Asians and Africans would have been even further impoverished. If Saudi Arabia had collapsed into chaos, then the Western economies would have been thrown into turmoil as oil prices doubled or trebled. As it was, the headline in the business section of *The Times* on 7 August 1990 was, "We have seen the last of cheap oil". Similarly, Denis Healey and Zbigniew Brzezinski predicted that the outbreak of war would send the price of oil up to $65 dollars a barrel, when it actually helped it to fall below $20.[53] If the conflict had developed into a Third World War with the use of nuclear weapons, as some of the pessimists believed, then the most important strategic taboo built up since 1945 would have been broken, with incalculable consequences for the future of humanity. Issues of great moment were at stake. But the fears expressed at the outset of the allies' military intervention were extreme and, in most respects, exaggerated.

Sources of Bias

Wishes or fears often (though by no means always) decisively influence what purport to be "scientific" or "expert" predictions. Some Moslem experts in the West, such as Dr Kalim Siddiqi or the "National Muslim Conference (UK)", which met in Bradford in January 1991, were deeply hostile to Western society.[54] They saw the coalition as a thinly veiled means of reasserting Western supremacy. When President Bush called for the overthrow of Saddam Hussein, one writer suggested that he "has confirmed the fears of many Arabs that the Americans are, in fact, bent upon the crushing of Iraq on Israel's behalf".[55] Many disliked the Kuwaiti and Saudi royal families. They opposed Israel's policies on the West Bank and saw the

United States as the main pillar of Israeli security. Thus they wanted the conservative Arab governments to collapse before the wrath of their people.

In the event their forecasts proved premature to say the least. They underestimated the strength of the conservatives and the sympathy and respect of Arab peoples for the West. Certainly Western values challenge many fundamental aspects of Moslem society. Professor von Laue has rightly pointed out that "the major effect of the world revolution of Westernisation...has been to undermine and discredit all non-Western cultures. The victorious Westerners...left the rest of the world humiliated and in cultural limbo".[56] Intellectuals, and particularly those comfortably ensconced in academic posts in Europe and the USA may feel deeply resentful of the West but other Moslems envy it for its democratic traditions and humanitarian aspirations.

It is very important in the context of these arguments to clarify what Western leaders hoped and expected from the war. The myth is already spreading that they knew it would be a "turkey shoot" from the very beginning. Yet the evidence shows that this was far from the case. If the coalition had realised that Iraqi forces would collapse so quickly, they would not have sent so many troops, at great expense, to Saudi Arabia. Equally, as has already been mentioned, many media commentators were far from confident about the outcome.

Western Public Opinion

During the Gulf conflict Western politicians had to make calculations both about the outcome and about public opinion in their own countries, and the contrasts between one country and another were extreme. In Germany the public seemed hostile to the war while the Japanese attitude appeared to be one of hostility or indifference. In Britain, by contrast, immediately after the Iraqi invasion between 83 and 87 per cent of the population supported the sending of British troops to the region.[57] The British government, therefore, enjoyed very broad support including that of most of the press. US public opinion seemed more uncertain in the early stages, but became more resolute as events developed. In August 1990, 52 per cent were opposed to taking action against Iraq which might lead either to increases in the price of petrol or to war. Even in early November of the same year, only 49 per cent thought that Kuwait was worth fighting for and headlines suggested that "American opinion (was) backing off war". Democratic Congressmen bitterly criticised the Administration for rushing into war, whilst newspapers described policy as "under a cloud of confusion".[58]

It was very difficult for the President and his advisers to manage the crisis and to deal with so many different constituencies. They had to appease Congress, the American public and armed forces as well as their Western allies, such as Britain and France, the pro-coalition Arab states and the Soviet Union. Yet as US policy became firmer and clearer at the end of November, the percentage in favour of using force if necessary rose by ten per cent.[59] Early in November *Time* magazine criticised President Bush for "spreading confusion about his plans". After the war was over it made him "man of the year". It seems likely that public opinion responded favourably to firm leadership. The Thatcher government in Britain took a very hard line from the start and was rewarded with massive public support (although the British victory against Argentina in 1982 may have encouraged the public to feel more confidence in its armed forces than was the case in the USA). The French line was more uncertain and it was only later in the crisis that the French people fully accepted the use of force. Afterwards newspaper reports compared Mitterand's prestige and popularity with that of de Gaulle.[60] Publics were willing to follow their governments whilst all went well, but there would have been a reaction (as in the Vietnam war) if the wrong political and military calculations had been made and the coalition had suffered defeats. The stakes were very high.

Western leaders certainly made crucial mistakes. Before the Iraqis invaded Kuwait, the US Ambassador in Baghdad told their leader that the State Department had asked her to say that Washington sympathised with his problems and had no opinion on border disputes between Arab states. There could hardly have been a worse signal to give to Saddam Hussein. Similar mistakes had been made by the then US Secretary of State, Dean Acheson before the outbreak of the Korean war when he gave the impression that the United States would not necessarily defend South Korea. Confusion about British intentions in the 1930s, and again before the Argentine invasion of the Falklands in 1982, might also be cited as examples of situations in which aggression by dictators was inadvertently encouraged by the apparent lack of will of a democratic government. The reasonable and understandable desire of such governments for accommodation is rarely matched by clarity about the bounds of their tolerance.

Miscalculations about the strength of the Iraqi regime were equally serious. Just as many Moslem commentators expected the conservative Arab regimes to collapse if war broke out, so the US administration appears to have believed that the Baghdad government would be overthrown after a military defeat. Thus it encouraged the Kurds in the north of Iraq and the Shiites in the south to rise against the Iraqi leader. Certainly governments have collapsed after less severe military defeats: the Greek junta fell after the Turks invaded Cyprus in 1974 and the Argentine junta did not long survive its defeat in 1982. But this is not an invariable consequence of defeat in war for an authoritarian regime: Nasser was not overthrown after his army's humiliation at Israeli hands in 1967.

Yet the coalition governments appear to have had no contingency plans to deal with the situation which arose when the Iraqi government defeated the rebels and set about destroying them. Had they recalled that control of the capital is usually the vital factor in a civil war and

41

that Saddam Hussein's secret police and some of his army were still intact, they might have been better prepared. In the event they dissipated much of the credit they had accrued for their military success in the war. Significantly, the proportion of British people satisfied with the way the US Administration was handling the crisis fell from 76 per cent in March 1991 to 45 per cent a month later.[61]

It is unclear whether threats by terrorist organisations of the mayhem they would create in the event of war were bravado from the start or whether they were thwarted by Western and Syrian preventive measures. They supported Saddam Hussein because he appeared to be standing up for the Palestinians and the Arab world as a whole against the United States. They also wanted to prove their power, but while they had a devastating effect on certain segments of the Western economies, particularly airlines and tourism, they had no impact on the outcome of the war itself.

CONCLUSION

The Western pessimists did not want to see Kuwait destroyed, the environment damaged or nuclear weapons used. They simply took a very gloomy view of the military balance and of the possibility of limiting modern warfare. They also expected that if war broke out it would be prolonged and it is true that, in general, the main reason why statesmen involve their countries in military disasters is because they wrongly expect to achieve swift victories. Very few plan for, or expect, prolonged campaigns, though in this case that may have been the best outcome that Saddam Hussein could hope for. The expectation that the war would be long was based on the assumed strength of the Iraqis and mistaken analogies with Vietnam and Korea where the terrain was completely different.[62] There was also great scepticism about the US armed forces and particularly their most modern, but untried, equipment. Fortunately conventional wars between advanced states are rare in the modern world. Whole ranges of equipment may enter service, take part in manoeuvres for ten or twenty years and then be sold or scrapped without ever being used in combat. Alternatively equipment may be employed for purposes quite different from those for which it was designed. Thus US B-52 strategic bombers were used to bomb Vietnamese guerrillas and Iraqi Republican Guards, not the Soviet cities and ports for which they were designed. But all this only adds to the difficulty of predicting how effective equipment will be in particular conflicts.

As events turned out, serving officers and officials came out of the conflict with a better reputation for predicting the course of military events than many outside experts.

43

Of course there were exceptions: Professor Halliday of the London School of Economics was already predicting in September 1990 that the allies would begin the use of force on 15 February the following year.[63] Many of the outside experts were, however, surprised by the outcome. This was a far cry from the Vietnam War during and after which many claimed that military leaders, politicians and officials had led the United States to disaster. Part of the reason was that conventional warfare depends on technology and tactics to a greater degree than guerrilla warfare. Very few outside commentators claimed to be experts on technology and those, like Professor Luttwak, who did make such a claim, proved to be totally misguided.

Academics and journalists are sometimes more sensitive to political issues than the military or officials, and politics largely determined the outcome of the Vietnam War. Yet this was not the only reason why the academics' record was inferior in the Gulf for, in the latter crisis, many academic experts miscalculated the political as well as the military issues. Professor Howard acknowledged that he had misjudged American opinion. Many others miscalculated the political situation in the Gulf. Edward Heath, Zbigniew Brzezinski, Denis Healey and others opposed the use of force because it might destroy Kuwait, lead to an ever expanding war including the use of nuclear weapons, damage the environment and cause the overthrow of the conservative Arab regimes. Some, at least, of these pessimistic forecasts - political and military - were always likely to be mistaken.

Nevertheless, because such forecasts were usually unfounded during the Gulf conflict, it is by no means certain that future wars will follow the same pattern. The coalition forces had the crucial advantage of months to work out their strategy, to co-ordinate their forces and to make it as certain as possible that all their equipment was operating effectively. It is unlikely that they would be given as much time in future and the performance of their equipment might well suffer in consequence. Moreover, the deliberate destruction of the Kuwaiti oil fields by Iraqi forces does set a precedent for countries to use any weapons, however damaging to the environment, if they think that this will serve their ends. Admittedly the Iraqi Army did not use chemical weapons against the coalition, presumably because they reckoned correctly that such weapons would be ineffective. But they can not be relied upon to abstain from the use of nuclear weapons, if they ever come into their possession and they think there is advantage in so doing. The pessimists could be right next time.

Experts can usually be expected to be both more knowledgeable and more biased than lay people. Soviet commentators, for example, were bound to be influenced by the fact that the Iraqis were using their equipment and emulating their tactics. Pacifists mustered all the arguments that they could think of against the use of force; terrorists and experts on terrorism stressed the vital importance that this might play if war broke out and environmentalists argued that potential damage to the environment was the crucial factor. None of this implies that their views could be ignored, only that they should be treated with appropriate caution.

Power takes many forms in the modern world and different types of power tend to vary in importance from conflict to conflict. Many observers had become used to the idea that Western states find it difficult to combat state-sponsored terrorism. The threat of terrorism during conventional conflicts was consequently exaggerated. Others over-estimated the significance of economic power and were surprised when the world's two most dynamic economic powers, Japan and Germany, proved impotent during the Gulf War.

The conflict, in fact, underlined the fractured nature of power in the modern world and its diffusion internationally. In retrospect we can see that the period after the Second World War was exceptional because the United States was not only the greatest industrial and financial power by far, but it also had the largest navy and the most sophisticated nuclear forces. American films and music dominated popular taste, and two of the three main international news agencies were American. The only challenges to American supremacy came from the Soviet Army, from the ideological pull which Moscow still exerted and from the power of national insurgencies modelled on Mao Tse Tung's victory in China.

Neither in the Nineteenth Century nor in the inter-war period was there such a concentration of power and influence as Washington amassed after 1945. In the Victorian age there were some five or six European powers with approximately equal strength. Britain had naval and industrial power; French was still the language of diplomacy and Paris the cultural centre; Germany and Russia had growing military and economic power. In 1918 the democracies emerged victorious from the First World War but Britain and France had accumulated vast debts and Britain, in particular, never recovered her pre-war economic pre-eminence. The United States was much the greatest economic power from then onwards, though it refused to take up all the responsibilities which this brought with it. Japan and the United States challenged British naval power, whilst communism, democracy and fascism competed for ideological supremacy. Power was so dispersed and its distribution changed so rapidly, that it proved impossible to preserve international stability.

Today socialism is as discredited as fascism. The ideological challenge to the democracies comes from the Moslem world; hence the effort which the coalition had to make in order to prevent Saddam Hussein presenting the Gulf conflict as a simple struggle between the West and Islam. Its economic predominance largely gone, the United States accepted reality by going "cap in hand" to the Germans and Japanese for funding for the war with Iraq - which would have been inconceivable in the Korean or Vietnamese Wars. Dozens of savage and destructive wars, from Southern Africa to Afghanistan and from East Timor to Peru prove that insurgency is as powerful as ever. But it is difficult to find any state which benefits from this process as the Chinese and Soviets were thought to do in the 1950s and 1960s.

Developments in an increasingly unstable world are going to put a premium on the ability to create coalitions to deal with crises as they arise. Nor will we have long to wait before such coalitions are needed - the growing instability in Eastern Europe and the Soviet Union, the chaos in much of Africa, the poverty in the Third World - will all challenge international statesmanship. In the Kuwaiti case, thanks to American leadership, Japanese and German economic power supported US, British and French conventional strength; Syrian expertise in terrorism apparently helped the coalition to keep terrorist movements at bay, while Chinese and Soviet votes in the Security Council helped to legitimise the actions of the coalition and ensure their acceptability to world opinion. The co-operation of all these countries gave economic sanctions such force as they possessed. One cannot assume that any of these circumstances will be replicated in a future conflict. Nor is it certain that a future coalition would be led with as much determination as the United States showed in the Gulf. A war which baffled so many of the experts is thus an appropriate introduction to the new international system which will replace the stability and predictability that the northern hemisphere, at least, has enjoyed for the last four decades.

NOTES

[1] "Bishop attacks 'victory' plans", *The Independent*, 4 March 1991. For conventional Arab views on the crisis see R. Hollis, "An Arab hero defying the world", *The Times*, 11 August 1991 and M. Heikal, "Out with the Americans, in with a new Arab order", *The Times*, 12 September 1990. For further examples of Siddiqi's views see "West's colonial war denounced", *The Independent*, 22 February 1991.

[2] Sir Michael Howard, "Why UN sanctions are better than a prolonged war", *The Times*, 17 August 1990 and "Gulf: no time for sanctions to bite", *The Times*, 2 January 1991.

[3] Paul Wilkinson, "A way to avoid the no-win war", *The Guardian*, 3 January 1991.

[4] See *The Military Balance 1989-1990*, International Institute for Strategic Studies, London, p.101. Figures for GDP are taken from the same source.

[5] V. Litovkin, "Weapons still unused", Novosti, from *Izvestia*, 28 January 1991. For fears of chemical and biological weapons, see "Germ war casualties would not go home", *The Independent*, 11 January 1991 and "A brief, lonely lesson in the masking of fear", *The Independent*, 17 January 1991. For the trenches full of oil see "Iraq plans to defend Kuwait with moat of burning oil", *The Times*, 31 December 1990.

[6] "Advocate for a nightmare scenario", *The Independent*, 20 December 1990. For the Scud missile see R. Pretty, *Jane's Pocket Book: Missiles*, Macdonald and Jane's, London, 1975, p. 193. See also "Scale of nuclear firepower threatens holocaust", *The Independent*, 15 January 1991.

[7] Raju Thomas, "The new balance of terror", *Trends Supplement* to *The Straits Times*, 31 January 1991.

[8] "Masked youths promise to redeem Iraqi leader", *The Times*, 14 August 1990; "Palestinians 'will retaliate' if the West attacks Iraq", *The Independent*, 19 September 1990; "Palestinians warn West of guerrilla retaliation", *The Times*, 24 September 1990.

[9] "Airline and travel industry facing worst recession ever", *The Times*, 2 February 1991; "Snow, Saddam and Slump send holiday bookings tumbling", *The Times*, 16 February 1991; "No place like home", *Time*, 11 February 1991. For the threats by deported Iraqi diplomats see "Expelled diplomats warn of reprisals if Iraq attacked", *The Times*, 5 January 1991, and for Iraqis interned in Britain see "Freed Iraqi internees may sue for false arrest", *The Independent*, 7 March 1991.

[10] "Syrian assurance kept terrorists at bay", *The Independent*, 4 March 1991.

[11] "Kuwait could burn for a year", *The Independent*, 3 January 1991. For Edward Heath's comments see "Advocate for a nightmare scenario", *The Independent*, 20 December 1990.

[12] "Kuwait is burning", *Time*, 18 March 1991.

[13] For Cheney's comments see "'Body-bag' count is anxious issue for US public", *The Independent*, 21 November 1990.

[14] "Captain with an eye on Saddam since college", *The Independent*, 31 August 1990.

[15] "Experts play down Saddam's 'shaky' front line", *The Times*, 22 August 1990.

[16] "Allies certain that Saddam's Maginot line can be broken", *The Times*, 24 November 1990.

[17] "Brigadier sees short and nasty campaign", *The Independent*, 20 February 1991.

[18] "US Army warned of 'massive casualties' if victory delayed", *The Independent*, 24 January 1991.

[19] "Warning on quality of Saddam's Army", *The Independent*, 7 November 1990.

[20] "Arithmetic of death in wake of Gulf War", *The Independent*, 20 March 1991.

[21] Edward Luttwak, "Blood for oil: Bush's growing dilemma", *The Independent*, 27 August 1990. For Luttwak's general position, see *Strategy: The Logic of War and Peace*, Harvard University Press, 1987. See also "Inside the high-tech arsenal", *Time*, 4 February 1991.

[22] For debates at the International Institute for Strategic Studies see Steven Canby, *New Technology and Western Security Policy*, Adelphi Paper number 198, London, 1985, p.7. For the "alternative" view of defence strategy see Johan Galtung in M. Clarke and M. Mowlam, *Debate on Disarmament*, Routledge and Kegan Paul, London, 1982; Mary Kaldor, *The Baroque Arsenal*, Abacus, London, 1982, p.2.

[23] "Heath warns of escalating war", *The Independent*, 12 December 1990.

[24] Elizabeth Young, letter to *The Independent*, 30 October 1990. For the Medical Campaign against Nuclear Weapons see letters in *The Independent*, 4 January 1991.

[25] Robert Fisk, "The dangerous command of General Disorder", *The Independent*, 3 December 1990; "A bloodless way", *The Independent*, 17 January 1991; "Hospitals brace themselves for the agony to come", *The Independent*, 21 January 1991. For criticisms of his reporting see letter from Colonel N. Fred in *The Independent*, 30 October 1990. Fred proved to be

very accurate in his predictions.

26 For Bogadanov's views see "Soviet general staff officer comments on Gulf War", Novosti, London, 5 February 1991. See also "Soviet military attack US policy", *The Independent*, 20 February 1991. For Kostin's views see "Land war is inevitable", Novosti from *Izvestia* of 7 February 1991.

27 For Filatov's views see "The Gulf War has not yet begun", Novosti from *Komsomolskaya Pravda*, 1 February 1991. "Soviet military on Gulf War lessons", Novosti from Tass report 1 March 1991. "Politicians and military vie to explain defeat", *The Times*, 2 March 1991.

28 "Top general fears use of force could provoke third world war", *The Independent*, 29 September 1990.

29 "Soviet military on Gulf War lessons", Novosti, *loc. cit.*

30 "Politicians and military vie to explain defeat", *The Times*, 2 March 1991.

31 "Serve the Soviet Union: an interview with Dmitri Yazov", Novosti from *Pravda*, 23 February 1991.

32 For Soviet delegations in Iraq see Edouard Volodin, "The Arab Knot", Novosti from *Sovietskaya Rossia*, 23 October 1990. For Soviet letters backing Iraq see, "I want to be a volunteer", *New Times*, 22-28 January 1991, p. 22.

33 "Arab generals predict one-day war", *The Times*, 31 December 1990; "Mubarak discounts tales of a long-drawn out war", *The Independent*, 17 January 1991.

34 "Excerpts from Iraqi transcript of meeting with US envoy", *New York Times International*, 23 September 1990.

35 "Bush hails defeat of Vietnam war syndrome", *The Times*, 2 March 1991.

36 For the views of the Iraqi Command Council see "Saddam says he can fight for years", *The Times*, 21 September 1990. See also "Iraqi people are braced for bitter battle", *The Independent*, 5 February 1991.

37 "Voice of Baghdad incites uprising", *The Times*, 14 August 1990. See also Rosemary Hollis, "An Arab hero defying the West", *The Times*, 11 August 1990.

38 "British Moslems show ambivalence", *The Independent*, 31 March 1990; The Pakistani Foreign Minister was forced to resign over the issue see "Gulf critics prompt Yaqub Khan to quit", *The Independent*, 28 February 1991.

39 "The perils of mocking Saddam", *The Times*, 1 October 1990; "PLO leader sees glimmer of hope amid encircling gloom", *The Independent*, 22 February 1991; "Kuwait Palestinians face gunmens' revenge", *The Independent*, 4 March 1991.

[40] "Denis Healey would not go to war", *The Independent*, 15 January 1991; M. Kaldor, "Time for mourning not rejoicing", *The Times*, 2 March 1991.

[41] "Trade embargo to bring shortages in Baghdad 'within a few weeks'", *The Times*, 8 August 1990; "Food the weakest link in Saddam defences", *The Times*, 13 August 1990; "Food supplies threatened as blockade begins to bite", *The Times*, 14 August 1990; "Iraqis well fed but hungry for cash", *The Independent*, 27 August 1990; "Sanctions bite, but Iraqis' diet seems sufficient", *The Independent*, 13 December 1990.

[42] "Iraqis confident as they count the cost of invasion", *The Independent*, 5 November 1990; "Iraq produces more, consumes less to survive", *The Independent*, 11 December 1990. For the UN's post war reports see "Iraqi people face catastrophe" and "UN report describes catastrophe", *The Independent*, 22 March 1991.

[43] For Cheney's comments on 15 December see "Cheney puts case for force as sanctions take time to bite", *The Times*, 15 December 1991.

[44] For the views of Douhet and others see P. Paret (Ed.), *The Makers of Modern Strategy*, Clarendon Press, Oxford, 1986, p. 624 *passim*. One of the best descriptions of the effects of bombing is John Terraine, *A Time for Courage*, Macmillan, New York, 1985. Historians often suggest that German morale was unbroken by bombing. This was not the case, the point was that the people could do nothing about bringing the war to an end.

[45] Philip Towle, *Pilots and Rebels*, Brassey's, London, 1989, p. 174 *passim*.

[46] "Puzzle of hit on French Embassy", *The Guardian*, 17 April 1986; "US massacre of civilians is an insult to us all", *The Guardian*, 17 April 1986.

[47] "Days of destruction, frustration and kindness under siege", *The Independent*, 9 February 1991 and "The myth of pinpoint bombing", *The Independent*, 14 February 1991. "RAF admits stray bomb hit town", *The Independent*, 18 February 1991.

[48] "Shelter a 'military target'", *The Independent*, 14 February 1991. See also "Days of destruction, frustration and kindness under siege", *The Independent*, 9 February 1991; "Baghdad rocked by rain of destruction", *The Independent*, 20 February 1991.

[49] "Deserters say Iraqi Army run by terror", *The Independent*, 14 November 1990; "Tiredness among troops swells the ranks of defectors", *The Independent*, 27 February 1991. For Luttwak's views on the bombing see "Supplies, not troops, should be target", *The Times*, 16 February 1991.

[50] Keith A. Dunn and William O. Staudenmaier, *Military Strategy in Transition: Defense and Deterrence in the 1980s*, US Army War College, un-

dated. For the war itself see "A 'perfect' victory is in sight", *The Independent*, 27 February 1991 and "Baptism of fire for air-land strategy", *The Independent*, 1 March 1991.

[51] Carl von Clausewitz, *On War*, Princeton University Press, New Jersey, 1984, pp. 85-86.

[52] For Mitterand, see "From President to hero", *The Independent*, 18 March 1991.

[53] "Denis Healey would not go to war", *The Independent*, 15 January 1991. For Brzezinski see Charles Krauthammer, "On getting it wrong", *Time*, 15 April 1991, p. 80.

[54] See note 1 *supra*. For the divisions within the British Moslem community see Clifford Longley, "Flight from the Mosque", *The Times*, 27 April 1991.

[55] Letter from Hidyat Zamani, *The Independent*, 28 February 1991.

[56] Theodore H. von Laue, *The World Revolution of Westernization*, Oxford University Press, New York, 1987, p. 5.

[57] "British Muslims show ambivalence", *The Independent*, 13 August 1990.

[58] For US opinion polls see *Time*, 20 August 1990 and 10 December 1990. For newspaper views of Bush see "Many faces of Bush confuse uneasy public", *The Times*, 31 December 1990; "US Gulf Policy under cloud of confusion", *The Independent*, 28 December 1990.

[59] For US polls in January see "Bush addresses nation in muted Churchillian tones", *The Independent*, 31 January 1991.

[60] See note 52 *supra*.

[61] See the opinion poll in *The Independent*, 26 April 1991.

[62] Sir Michael Howard, "Why UN sanctions are better than a prolonged war", *The Times*, 17 August 1990. See also Jeffrey Record, "Why Air War Worked", *Armed Forces Journal*, April 1991, p.44.

[63] "Analysts disagree on timing of conflict", *The Times*, 1 October 1990.

Occasional Paper No. 49

A FAREWELL TO ARMS CONTROL
The Irrelevance of CFE
by Christopher Coker

During the Cold War, arms control was seen in the West as a crucial means of maintaining peace. Yet the signing of the latest CFE treaty passed virtually unnoticed in the media despite the fact that many of its provisions broke new ground.

Dr. Christopher Coker of the London School of Economics analyses the reasons for this and concludes that the apparent easing of East-West tension has created a new "security environment" which has marginalised arms control in the European security debate.

While the West is reducing its forces to levels below those that they are permitted to retain by arms control agreements, there is little sign of the Soviet Union following suit. As war between West Europeans has become anachronistic, a similar process may, Dr. Coker argues, be under way in East-West relations.

**Price including postage £5.00 (UK/Europe); $9.00 (USA);
£6.00 (Other countries)**

European Security Study No. 11

CZECHOSLOVAKIA
Too Velvet A Revolution?
by James de Candole

Czechoslovakia's transition to democracy was so smooth that it is easy to overlook the problems which remain.

As James de Candole points out, the process of weeding out the old *nomenklatura* has been slow and this has hindered the transition to a market economy. Also, there is worrying evidence of the continuing influence of former members of the secret police, many of whom have kept up their old links with the KGB.

The traditional tensions between Czechs and Slovaks have been revived, threatening the country's fragile unity. Mr. de Candole questions the Havel government's conciliatory policy towards former communists, and suggests that *lustrace*, or vetting, of those in public life must be even more thorough if Czechoslovakia is to successfully face the challenge of rebuilding its economy and society.

**Price including postage £5.00 (UK/Europe); $9.00 (USA);
£6.00 (Other countries)**

Occasional Paper No. 48

RETREAT TO MOSCOW
Gorbachev and the East European Revolution
by Mark Almond

As the euphoria which surrounded the toppling of the Stalinist regimes of Eastern Europe in 1989 is dispelled, questions are now being posed about how spontaneous some of the uprisings were, and about the exact role which the Soviet Union played in the downfall of the old order.

President Havel of Czechoslovakia has already revealed that the "velvet revolution" there began with a KGB conspiracy and there is evidence of direct Soviet involvement in the collapse of the Honecker regime in East Germany.

Dr. Mark Almond, of Oriel College, Oxford, sifts the evidence and suggests that the Soviet objective in Eastern Europe was the installation of "reformed" communist, not democratic regimes there and suggests how the new revelations about the "Revolutions of 1989" should influence the West's attitude to President Gorbachev and *perestroika* and the formulation of future policy.

**Price including postage £5.00 (UK/Europe); $9.00 (USA);
£6.00 (Other countries)**

Occasional Paper No. 47

WHO ONLY ENGLAND KNOW:
Conservatives and Foreign Policy
by Christopher Coker

The Conservative Government's radical approach to domestic policy has not been matched in foreign affairs. As a result, Christopher Coker argues, Britain is in danger of drifting into irrelevance. Mrs Thatcher's attitude to European integration has left Britain increasingly isolated in the EC. The Commonwealth, meanwhile, has become an irrelevance - of no help either to Britain or her former dependencies as a means of facing post-imperial realities. Dr. Coker suggests that early hopes that capitalism at home would lead to a liberal external policy have been unfulfilled. Even though the Prime Minister has been firm in her support for democracy in Poland, for example, the "Know How" Fund designed to further it has been blunted by unimaginative Whitehall officials.

Dr. Coker urges a fundamental reappraisal of British interests and of the means of securing them, as the old certainties of foreign and defence policy dissolve with the end of the Cold War.

**Price including postage £5.00 (UK/Europe); $9.00 (USA);
£6.00 (Other countries)**

OTHER PUBLICATIONS IN PRINT